THE
Dolphin

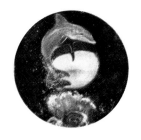

$\mathcal{P}$lease
visit the
Hay House
Website at:
http://www.hayhouse.com

THE
Dolphin

Story of a Dreamer

Sergio Bambaren

HAY
HOUSE

Hay House, Inc.
Carlsbad, CA

Copyright © 1994 by Sergio Bambaren
Revised Copyright © 1997

Illustrations © 1997 by Michele Gold

Published and distributed in the United States by:
Hay House, Inc., P.O. Box 5100, Carlsbad, CA 92018-5100
(800) 654-5126 • (800) 650-5115 (fax)

First published in Australia, May 1995

Edited by: Jill Kramer   Designed by: Christy Allison

Library of Congress Cataloging-in-Publication Data

Bambaren, Sergio.
     The dolphin : story of a dreamer / Sergio Bambaren;
illustrated by Michele Gold.
     p.   cm.
     ISBN 1-56170-391-5 (hardcover)
     1. Dolphins—Fiction.   I. Title.
PS3552.A47315D65   1997
813'.54—dc21   97-14212
                                    CIP

ISBN 1-56170-391-5

00 99 98 97   4 3 2 1
First Printing, Hay House, Inc., July 1997

Printed in the United States of America

To the dreamer within us all.

*May your dreams
come true, dreamer;
and may they always
bring you happiness
and wisdom.*

PART
ONE

The first rays of the morning sun filtered gently through the breaking clouds, unveiling the unspoiled beauty of a remote coral island, set like a jewel in the middle of a deep blue sea.

A tropical storm had just hit the area, and a huge swell was pounding the reef. The once-placid ocean had turned into a raging torrent of surf and spray.

Suddenly, when a huge wave was about to break, a young dolphin appeared from the deep, and crossing the wave as it hit the reef, he projected a thin trail across the wall of water, fighting hard to maintain an edge between bottom and crest, holding his breath...

The lip of the wave slowly wrapped him, deeper and deeper, taking him to a place surfers dream of: the barrel.

And then, as he finished cutting the face of the wave, the lone dolphin managed a beautiful cutback and exited the wave with a magnificent pull-out.

He decided that this would be the last wave he'd surf this morning, so he swam into the island's lagoon, exhausted, but happy.

Daniel Alexander Dolphin and the surf were inseparable. From watching the sun rise every morning, and set every afternoon, to all those surfing sessions in which he would forget the meaning of time, Daniel knew that there was nothing more important in his life than the moments he spent riding waves.

Indeed, more than anything else, Daniel Dolphin loved to surf. It was in his blood and in his soul, and it made him feel free. Surfing helped him achieve a unique communication

with the sea, making him realize that the ocean was not only a mass of moving water, but something alive, full of wisdom and beauty.

Daniel Dolphin was a dreamer. He was convinced that there was more to life than fishing and sleeping, so he had decided to devote all his energies to discovering the true purpose of his life through his surfing and the wisdom of the sea. That was his dream.

From the beginning, this way of thinking brought him problems with the pod. Many of his friends could not understand what he was trying to achieve.

Every morning, while getting ready to fish, the pod would watch Daniel head toward the reef, ready for another surfing session. How could he waste so much time doing something that would not help him find the food he needed? It was pure madness.

One evening, when Daniel was returning from the surf, Michael Benjamin Dolphin, Daniel's best friend, came to him and asked, "What do you think you're doing, Daniel? Why are you risking your life in the reef? What are you trying to prove?"

"I am not trying to prove anything," Daniel replied. "I just want to know what I can learn from the sea and my surfing. That's all."

"For heaven's sake, Daniel, a lot of dolphins who care about you think that sooner or later you will get killed. Riding waves was fun when we were calves, but now you are pushing yourself to the limit. Why don't you spend your time catching more fish instead of wasting it surfing the reef?"

Daniel Dolphin stared at his old friend, and after being quiet for a while, he said, "Michael, look around you. Our world is full

of dolphins that fish from dawn to dusk, one day after another. They are always fishing. They don't have the time to pursue their dreams anymore. Instead of fishing to live, they now live to fish."

Daniel's voice turned to the past. "I remember a young and strong Michael Dolphin who could stare at the waves for hours, imagining himself on top of one of those giant walls of water, dreaming. Now I only see a scared dolphin, always fishing, afraid of living his own dreams. What could be more important in life than to follow your dreams, whatever they are?"

Daniel stared at his friend and said, "Find time in your life to dream, Michael. Don't let your fears stand in the way of your dreams."

Michael was confused, knowing that what he had heard was true; but the idea of a life made of dreams was foreign to him. He was

not a calf anymore, and his dreams had been replaced by duties. Wasn't that why he fished? Besides, what would the other dolphins think if they saw him riding waves?

He remembered his days as a surfer as something that belonged to his youth, to the past. He had thought about surfing again, but he was so tired after fishing all day that he could always think of some good reason not to do it.

Michael looked at his friend Daniel, and trying to be convincing, said to him, "Someday, Daniel, you will grow up and see things the way the rest of the pod sees them. There is no other way." And then Michael was gone.

Daniel's sadness was evident, and although Michael had changed a lot since the times they had spent together surfing and discovering new, secret spots, he still loved him as he had

years before. He knew the joy they had shared was still in his heart, but for some reason, Michael had stopped dreaming.

Daniel's heart was aching, but he felt that there was nothing more he could do to help his friend. He knew he would be misunderstood for telling others what he felt inside, for trying to show them the freedom he experienced while surfing.

But Daniel Dolphin also knew that he would be hooked forever on the magic he had discovered, riding waves alone in the vastness of his beloved sea.

He had chosen to live his life based on his own principles, and although he was sometimes lonely, he had no regrets.

Daniel learned fast in the days and weeks that followed. He spent whole days surfing the reef, sometimes even forgetting to take time out to feed himself; and although he was happy with the life he had chosen, he wished he could share with the pod what he felt inside. "If I could only find a way to show them the freedom I feel when surfing," he said to himself, "maybe they would realize how important it is to follow your dreams. Then again, I don't have any right to interfere with their lives. Who am I to tell them what is wrong and what is right?

"That's it. From now on, I'll just try to be the best I can be. There are still lots of things I have to discover about my surfing, so I won't bother anyone anymore."

Daniel felt good about his decision. He would follow his dreams as he had always

done, for better or worse.

He was heading back to the lagoon when, suddenly, he heard a voice.

He could barely understand what was being said, but words were being whispered to him.

Who could it be?

In his confusion, Daniel lost his balance and almost got washed in to shore. Who was calling him? The voice sounded familiar, like someone he had always known. He looked around, but he was definitely alone.

He became afraid. Had the loneliness, the price paid for living his dreams, finally taken its toll? Was he mad?

And then he heard the voice once more. But this time, it was clear:

There comes a
time in life
when there is
nothing else to
do but go your
own way.
A time to
follow your
dreams. A time
to raise the
sails of your
own beliefs.

Daniel felt very uncomfortable. Someone was filtering his thoughts and searching his soul, discovering his innermost secrets.

"Who are you?" he asked.

"I am the voice of the sea."

"The voice of the sea?"

"Yes, Daniel. You have achieved something that other dolphins cannot even begin to imagine. All your hard work in the surf, all that time you have spent alone practicing, following your dream, has finally paid off."

And then Daniel Dolphin heard the words that would change his destiny forever:

"You have learned well, Daniel, and a new stage of your life will now begin, the one that holds the answers to your dream."

The voice was clear and strong. Daniel's initial fear had disappeared, and more than merely hearing the words, he was understanding them.

"I have been trying to communicate with you for some time, Daniel, trying to support you in times of weakness. Do not fear anymore. As long as you follow your dream, I will be here to help you. Trust your instincts, follow the omens in the life you have chosen to live, and you will fulfill your dream."

The voice began to fade.

"No, please wait!" Daniel pleaded. "There are things I need to know, like where do I go from here, or how will I know what to do, and how will I find the true purpose of my life?"

With the kindest voice Daniel had ever heard, the sea said, "Only this I can tell you, Daniel Alexander Dolphin: You will find the true purpose of your life the day you surf the perfect wave."

"The perfect wave? What do you mean by that? How will I find it?"

The sea spoke to Daniel's heart:

Falling into the
deepest despera-
tion gives you
the chance to
find your true
nature. Just as
dreams come
alive when you
least expect
them to, so will
the answers to
questions you
cannot unfold.
Let your instincts
build a trail of
wisdom, and let
your fears be
diminished by
hope.

"You have done well, Daniel," said the sea, "and now I must go."

The voice vanished.

It took some time for Daniel Dolphin to realize the nature of the gift he had just received. "The sea loves me as much as I love him," he told himself, "and has been sharing all those beautiful moments with me, just as I always felt I was sharing them with him. Now he will also show his wisdom to me."

This new understanding would certainly change the rest of his life.

Daniel didn't know where this revelation would take him, but he knew he wouldn't feel alone again. Not as long as he followed his dream....

That afternoon, Daniel swam back to the pod. All the dolphins were there, and as usual, they made fun of him. "Look," they said, "here comes the dolphin that never grew up. How many fish did you catch today, Daniel?"

But Daniel's thoughts were an eternity away. The sea had enlightened him with understanding, and now, more than ever, he knew he had to follow his dream, the one that would show him the real purpose of his life.

Some months had passed since Daniel Dolphin had heard the voice of the sea and realized that dreams were made to come true. By now his relationship with the sea had grown strong, and his surfing had

improved dramatically.

He had discovered that each wave he surfed, big or small, had its own essence, its own purpose. From a two-foot wave on a balmy day, to a ten-foot close-out at the peak of a storm, Daniel's attitude toward learning from each maneuver he tried to pull would be the same, and instead of becoming disappointed when he failed, he would try to make the best of it by identifying his errors and trying to correct them in the next wave.

One day, in a classic six-foot swell with offshore winds, he had learned a lesson from the sea after losing a wave in a miserable way.

Most of us are
not prepared
to overcome
our failures,
and because
of this we are
not able to
fulfill our
gifts. It is easy
to stand for
something that
does not carry
a risk.

So Daniel would put into practice what the sea had taught him. His surfing improved, and a new lesson was learned.

Daniel Dolphin used this same knowledge to face the difficulties he encountered in life, and he discovered that things turned out better.

He knew in his heart that all the things he shared with the sea were the means to achieve something more important, spiritually much higher than anything he had seen or experienced before. He was looking for that perfect wave, the one that would come some day to show him the true purpose of his life.

So Daniel tried in the days that followed to understand where his dream was taking him. Instead of just trying to surf well, he would also listen to his heart every time he mastered a new technique that gave more

freedom to his movements. He tried hard, paying attention to every detail.

He had started experimenting on the outer reef, a region of the island beyond which no dolphin had ventured, a place forbidden by the Law of the pod.

And just when desperation was about to make him quit, he remembered what the sea had said:

"There comes a time in life, when there is nothing else to do but go your own way..."

He recalled the first time he had heard this revelation from the sea, but now understanding lit Daniel's heart, and he realized what the sea had been trying to tell him. He understood what all the practice, all the hours improving his technique, increasing his confidence and strength had been for.

He had to take the big leap into the unknown, far away from the safety of his

reef—a place in the world where the rules that governed the pod no longer had significance or value. In order to find the real purpose of his life, Daniel Dolphin had to set aside everything that limited him.

"Now I understand!" he said, and there was triumph in his voice. "The perfect wave will not come to me. I will have to find *it!*"

This new revelation brought back memories to Daniel. He remembered being a calf, hearing the elder dolphin speak about leaving the reef. In a formal and ceremonial voice, he had said:

"Thou shall not abandon the inner reef of our world. It has been there since the beginning of times and has always protected us from the danger that exists beyond. We must respect this divine decision by accepting the Law."

It's funny, Daniel thought. He had learned to respect the elder dolphin and his beliefs, and at the same time to live his life based on his own principles and the lessons learned from the sea. Would the elder dolphin respect him for taking a decision that would break the whole system that ruled the pod's existence?

Daniel didn't think so.

So that night, he decided not to tell anyone what he was going to do or where he was heading. Secretly and silently, he would leave the pod as he had always done when going for a late surfing session. But this time, he would not return. The pod would think that, as they had predicted, he had drowned. He had paid with his life for not following their advice. Everyone would talk about the consequences of not following the Law, of breaking the rules.

The day Daniel Dolphin left his beloved reef was a day he would never forget.

He had been preparing for his departure and was sure he had taken care of every detail. The only sadness that touched his heart was the thought that in the middle of all those strangers that made up the pod, some dolphin could be saddened by the news of his alleged death, believing in his heart that maybe, and only maybe, crazy Daniel was right. This made him think that he should stay a little longer, just in case there was someone like him, also trying to find a higher purpose in life, just maybe...?

Maybe part
of loving is
learning
to let go,
knowing when
to say good-
bye. Not letting
our feelings
get in the way
of what will
probably,
in the end, be
better for
the ones we
care for.

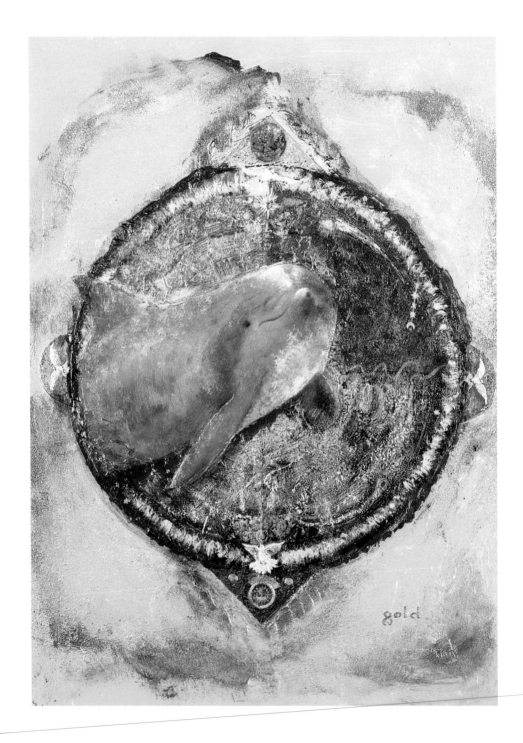

gold

So that evening, Daniel started to swim toward the outer reef, with no witness but the full moon up in the sky, the fulfillment of his dream as his only destiny. He felt a little scared, but there was beauty in having his fear under control. "It's such a lovely night," he said. "What could possibly go wrong?"

He felt good about himself because, whatever happened, he was the maker of his own destiny.

That night Daniel had to fight not only against tides and rips, but against his own doubts. "The hard work starts now," he told himself. And he found out that all those solitary sessions of surfing and all that mental and physical preparation had given him the strength to face not only the most awesome wave, but also his own destiny.

PART TWO

*T*he next morning, Daniel Alexander Dolphin found himself in the middle of a huge ocean, not knowing which way to go, but willing to be guided.

He was overwhelmed by the size of the ocean beyond his little island. There was no reef or land in sight. He felt a little apprehensive. Now that he had come this far and pushed himself to the limit, what next? Was this all there was?

Even so, he felt at peace with the decision he had taken. The fear he experienced while swimming beyond the reef had subsided, and now, in the vastness of his solitude, he knew that his life was heading in the right direction, toward a place he had always known existed, but one he had never seen or experienced before.

Daniel was submerged in all these

thoughts when suddenly, a huge mass of water thrown by some formidable force erupted at his side on the surface. Amid the shower of water, he saw something huge, something ten times his size. He realized that the slightest physical contact would crush him.

Never had he seen anything like this, but he did not feel threatened or scared; in fact, it felt strangely like the arrival of some old friend, unexpected, but welcome.

"Who are you?" Daniel asked.

"I am a humpback whale." The gentle giant kept swimming.

Daniel had to swim fast just to stay close.

"What are you doing?" Daniel asked.

"I am migrating. I have to reach warmer waters before the arrival of winter." She turned toward Daniel. "And you, what are you doing in the middle of the ocean?"

"I am following a dream," Daniel said. "I

left my pod and my island some time ago, and am searching for the perfect wave, the one that will show me the true purpose of my life."

"I respect you for your decision," the whale said. "It must be hard to leave your world to follow a dream."

She looked at Daniel. "You must be very careful in this journey on which you have embarked. Pay attention to everything you do or see, and you will learn many things. It's not only getting to your destiny, but also the journey itself that will show you the meaning of the perfect wave and how to find it."

"Your wisdom is great," Daniel said, "and I thank you for sharing it with me." He was about to ask the whale which direction to take when a black silhouette appeared on the horizon. It seemed to sit on top of the water, throwing smoke and ashes into the air.

"What is that?" Daniel asked.

The whale started to shiver. Suddenly her expression changed to one of fear, and without notice she started to swim away at great speed.

How can such a gentle giant be so afraid? What could frighten someone so big? Daniel wondered. He couldn't help feeling very sad, and a little scared.

Daniel caught up with the whale and asked if he could help, but the gentle giant kept swimming. However, before leaving, she said, "Beware of a creature called man."

"What do you mean?" Daniel asked. "I don't know anyone by that name. In my island, besides some friendly seagulls, we are all dolphins."

"Beware of a creature called man." Those were her last words.

"Is man a bad dolphin?" Daniel asked himself.

He felt that the sea was about to speak, so he kept very quiet, listening.

Discovering new
worlds will not
only bring you
happiness and
wisdom, but also
sadness and fear.
How could you
value happiness
without knowing
what sadness is?
How could you
achieve wisdom
without facing your
own fears? In the
end, the great
challenge in life
is to overcome
the limits within
yourself, pushing
them to places you
would never have
dreamed they
could go.

This first encounter with something that did not belong to his island made Daniel understand that the world was not as small as he had been told. He realized that his ignorance was a result of having believed what he had been taught, without even asking where the information had come from.

This journey would help Daniel Dolphin to expand the horizons of his world, discovering things that the pod would never have even dreamed existed!

Daniel Dolphin continued traveling through his beloved sea for thirty days and thirty nights. He traveled from dawn to dusk, always trusting his instincts, trying to find the omens that the sea had promised would

guide him toward his destiny.

He again noticed the black smoke on the horizon. Although he remembered the whale's fear, he decided to investigate.

He approached the silhouette and noticed that the water around it was unclear and dirty. An oily film started to stick to his skin. He also noticed dead fish floating by. The horror of this almost made him ill.

At first he couldn't believe his eyes; the huge thing was somehow, by means of some kind of net, dragging all the fish out of the sea. Some he recognized as the ones his pod relied on in order to survive, but others were not safe to eat!

In disbelief, Daniel also saw some dead dolphins being thrown back into the ocean.

How could this be possible? Who was the senseless creature performing this act of death?

And then he remembered his encounter with the whale:

"Beware of a creature called man."

Could this being be part of the evil the elder dolphin had said existed beyond the reef?

"From here on," Daniel told himself, "I shall be very careful."

The next morning Daniel was resting. He had been traveling all night, trying to get as far away as he could from the black silhouette that drained the sea of all forms of life.

He was about to restart his journey when he noticed the presence of a strange fish that forced its head out of the water toward the sun.

"Who are you?" Daniel asked.

"They call me 'sunfish,'" the fish replied.

That's a funny name, Daniel thought.

"What do you do, sunfish?"

"I sleep at night and I follow the sun during the day. I've been trying to touch it every day of my life, with no luck. But I know I will, someday."

"Is that your dream?" Daniel asked.

"Yes," said the sunfish. "I have always dreamed of how warm the sun must be to keep this whole world alive."

"I don't think you will ever be able to touch the sun," Daniel said. "You were born to live in the sea, and if you try to get out of it, you will certainly die."

"Every morning," said the sunfish, "the sun rises on the horizon, regardless of what I do. I can feel its warmth, and its warmth reminds me of my dream. What would you do in my position? Would you abandon your dream for fear of dying, or would you try to touch the sun?"

There was no way Daniel could lie to this magnificent creature. "I would try to touch the sun," he said.

"Then," the sunfish replied, "I'll die trying to realize my dream. At least that's better than dying without following it." He stared at Daniel. "Do you have a dream?"

"Yes. To find the perfect wave, the one that will show me the real purpose of my life when I ride it," Daniel said, and a strange light shone in his eyes.

"That's quite a dream," said the sunfish, "and I think I can help you. In my voyages through the sea, I have noticed that the swells always come from the west, pushed by strong winds blowing from the confines of the ocean. It is there that you will find the wave you are searching for. Just wait until the sun is about to set, and follow it in its journey toward the sea."

Daniel thanked the sunfish. He was happy for having learned so much this day.

We all have dreams, he thought. The only difference is that some fight and persevere to reach their destiny, no matter what the risks are. Others simply ignore their dreams, afraid of losing what they've got. They never realize what the true purpose of their life is.

As advised by the sunfish, Daniel kept traveling toward the west, always heading where the sun and the sea met at dusk, because he knew in his heart that the sunfish was one of the omens the sea had said he would have to follow.

Daniel Dolphin had no problem traveling after sunset. Thousands of years of evolution had provided him with night vision. He could emit high-pitched sounds that bounced off objects in front of him. In this way, he could decipher the echo signal that

rebounded to him, producing an image from the sound waves. Daniel was able to perceive objects in the darkness of the night and in the depths of the ocean.

He was heading west when he sensed a figure in front of him. He approached the creature carefully.

"Who are you?" Daniel asked.

"I am a shark, and you shouldn't be talking to me. We can hurt dolphins. You should be scared of me."

"I don't fear what I don't know," Daniel said.

The shark hesitated. No dolphin had ever replied to him.

"Well, you should be careful in the open sea," the shark said. "Where is the rest of your pod?"

"I'm sure they must be fishing in the safety of the island's lagoon," Daniel answered.

"So what are you doing alone, so far from the pod?"

"I am following my dream. I am looking for the perfect wave."

"And where will you find it?" asked the shark.

"I'm not sure. I just know I am heading in the right direction." He stared at the shark. "Are you a dreamer, too?"

"I used to be one," the shark said, and his voice was filled with sadness. "Life has been unfair to me. It has made everyone fear me. Every time I appear, all other creatures swim for their lives."

"It reminds me of my pod," Daniel said. "Every time a storm hits the island, they swim for shelter, inside the lagoon. It is fear of the unknown that makes them behave that way. They don't realize that the most beautiful lessons in life are learned in the toughest

situations."

"You are not scared of me," said the shark.

"I am not scared of you, because if you wanted to kill me, you could have done so. But most of all, I am not afraid of you because I am following my dream, because I know I have to reach my destiny."

"I wish I could dream like you," the shark said.

"Well then, start dreaming again. Just remember when you were young. Remember the special thoughts that would steal your sleep at night."

"What happens if I don't remember how to dream?" the shark asked.

"When you want something with all your heart," Daniel said, "there is nothing that can stop you but your own fears."

"Are you saying I can dream again?"

"Just like any other creature in this world," Daniel answered.

"Thank you," said the shark. "I shall dream again." He was about to leave, but turned and asked, "Did you say you were looking for the perfect wave?"

"Yes," said Daniel.

"Well, you could be getting very close. I have just come from the west, and I have seen a swell building up. Maybe the wave you are searching for is part of that swell."

"Follow the omens," the sea had said.

"How can I get there?" Daniel asked.

"Just keep going west and trust your instincts," said the shark. "And listen to your heart, 'cause it knows all you need to fulfill your dream."

At this stage, Daniel was missing his surfing more than ever. He had started to feel sad in a world of strangers, not knowing if he would ever see his beautiful island again. He had thought that the world would be a place full of beautiful surprises, and although he had seen lots of them, he had also seen some unpleasant ones.

It was one of those moments when he felt like returning to his lagoon.

But, as promised, the sea was there to help him.

Perhaps dreams are
made of lots of hard
work. Perhaps if we
try to cut corners,
we lose track of
the reason we started
dreaming, and at the
end we find that
the dream no longer
belongs to us. Perhaps
if we just follow the
wisdom from our
heart, then time
will make sure we
get to our destiny.
Remember: When you
are just about to give
up, when you feel that
life has been too hard
on you: Remember
who you are.
Remember your
dream.

Daniel felt good knowing that as long as he kept working to fulfill his dream, he would never be alone. So he kept swimming, trying to find a place to rest.

Daniel saw an old dolphin coming from the west. He was swimming peacefully, in the vastness of a gentle blue sea.

Daniel Dolphin swam toward him.

The old dolphin noticed Daniel's presence. "What is your name?" he asked softly.

"I am Daniel Alexander Dolphin."

"And what are you doing alone in the middle of the ocean, Daniel Dolphin?"

"I am following my dream."

The old dolphin's expression quickly changed. "Are you the one looking for the

perfect wave?" he asked. The words were strong and calm.

Daniel couldn't believe what he was hearing. "How do you know that?"

"The same way we both know that there is more to life than to fish and sleep," he said. The old dolphin's voice broke.

"Why are you crying?" Daniel asked, puzzled.

The old dolphin stared at Daniel. "I am crying because I am happier than I've ever been. After all these years, I have finally realized my dream."

"What do you mean?" Daniel asked, without understanding.

"I was once as young and strong as you, Daniel," he said. "I was a dreamer like you, long ago, with questions about life that would steal my sleep."

"What happened?"

"One day I stopped dreaming. I followed the Law of the pod instead of following my heart. And I started to feel old." The old dolphin continued, "We start to become wiser as we age. And the day came when I realized that it was time for me to follow my dream, although I was not sure if I would be able to achieve it. I had wasted too much time in my life, and I was feeling tired. But I also felt that I couldn't stay with the pod anymore, so I decided to follow my dream anyway.

"I started my journey many years ago," the old one said, "and I learned that the younger you start to trust your heart, the easier it is to follow your dreams.

"Some time ago," the old dolphin continued, "I was traveling through the ocean, my thoughts more confused than ever, thinking that the idea of following my dream at such an old age had been a mistake and that it

would have been better for me to stay with the pod and wait for my death." He stared at the sky. "I was about to quit and return, when I heard a voice." He turned to Daniel. "I suspect you have heard it, too."

"Yes," said Daniel. He felt happy that for the first time in his life he could share his secret with someone who would not make fun of him. "The voice of the sea..."

"Yes!" exclaimed the old dolphin, and he nearly burst with joy. "He told me that it is better to follow your dreams no matter how old you are, than not to follow them at all." He took a deep breath. "Now I can go in peace," he said, and a magical glow surrounded him.

"You haven't told me what your dream is," Daniel said.

The old one looked at Daniel. "My dream was to meet a young dolphin who would

make me remember when I was a dreamer," he said, "and to tell him not to let his chance in life slip away, no matter what the odds are. And to help him fulfill his dream."

"What do you mean?" Daniel asked. "How will you help me fulfill my dream?"

"I have come from the west, Daniel Dolphin," he said, "and I have seen the swell in which you will surf the perfect wave, the one that will show you the real purpose of life. In all my travels, I have never seen anything that could even resemble what you are about to experience, very soon."

He turned and Daniel saw his eyes. They were shining like stars in the sky.

"It's not a huge swell," the old dolphin said, "but it will be very special for you...."

PART THREE

*I*t was at sunset on the fortieth day since Daniel had left his island that he heard a familiar sound. He started to feel excited. Could it be what he thought it was?

It had been a long time since he had sensed that magic, so he swam toward the place where the roar was coming from.

He couldn't believe his eyes. Two hundred feet away from him, the most awesome reef break he had ever seen was spitting perfect barrels, one after another.

He couldn't guess at the size of the waves, but his experience told him that it was a very respectable swell. Without hesitation, Daniel swam toward the break and caught a wave. Before night had fallen, he had managed to ride a couple. This made him feel alive again!

In his excitement, Daniel did not realize

where he had landed. The reef was an extension of some enormous cliffs, some kind of island larger than anything he had seen before.

Daniel also noticed that, as dusk covered the sky, hundreds of lights had started to illuminate the island's coast. Some of them were still, while others were moving in a line, sometimes disappearing and then appearing again. This really caught him by surprise. He was used to the darkness of the night and had learned to love the moon and the stars shining in the sky. He was a little bit annoyed that all those tiny lights dimmed the stars and the moon.

It had been a long day, and Daniel was very tired. He wouldn't try to find out what those lights were until the next day. The important thing now was to sleep well and have a great surfing session first thing in the morning.

Daniel smiled. "I feel about surfing tomorrow the same way I felt when surfing for the first time, so long ago. I have surfed ten thousand times and will probably surf ten thousand times more. I know I will never get tired of it, but why?"

There are some
things you cannot
see with your eyes.
You have to see
them with your
heart, and that is
the hard part of
it. For instance,
if you find the
spirit of the young-
ster inside of you,
with your memo-
ries and his
dreams, you two
will walk together,
trying to find a
way through this
adventure called
life. Always trying
to make the best of
it. And your heart
will never become
tired, or old...

If we could all feel the same way about the things we do, then our lives would have more meaning, Daniel thought.

That night Daniel went to sleep as dreamers do, looking to the future with excitement, his heart bursting with joy.

He knew that tomorrow would be a great day of surfing, then he knew nothing more.

He was instantly asleep.

He woke up with the sun's first rays.

At first glance, the place he had discovered the night before seemed very different from the place he was staring at. Although the lights were not there, huge constructions were standing at the edge of the cliffs. He could sense movement, so he guessed that

some kind of living creature had built them.

Should he try to find out what was going on?

Definitely not, he decided. He had come this far with one purpose: to discover who he was and where he was heading, to find the purpose of his life through the perfect wave. That was his dream. So, as planned the night before, he headed toward the reef for his first surfing session in this magical place he had found.

Although the swell had probably peaked the night before, there were still plenty of waves to ride. There was a sweet offshore breeze, the water was warm, and so was the air. With this six-foot swell, the conditions were perfect.

Daniel caught his first wave and found that it jacked up very fast before breaking hollow in the shallow take-off. He had to be very careful not to hit the reef. He would

catch the next wave very early, dropping sideways. The first section was very fast, and he had to swim hard to beat it. Then the wave turned into a solid but slow wall that could be used for radical cut-backs and re-entries. At the end, the last tubey section turned into a close-out that wrapped him, making him feel part of the sea....

The whole experience was magical, and it was the reason why Daniel would lose all sense of time when he was surfing. He would just swim back to the take-off and keep catching waves until he was totally exhausted.

Daniel Dolphin felt happier than he had for a long time. He had finally found a real prize for his endeavor, and now, more than ever, he felt he had made the right decision in leaving the pod and the island in order to broaden his horizons.

Decisions are
a way of
defining
ourselves.
They are the
way to give
life and
meaning to
words, to
dreams.
They are the
way to let
what we are
be what we
want to be.

The hours flew by, and although Daniel did not notice how long he had been surfing, he did start to feel tired, so he decided to get a last wave before resting.

Daniel took off on his last wave, but suddenly, before finishing the take-off, he lost his concentration and fell into the wave's wall. He knew what was coming.

The lip of the wave caught him and threw him against the rock bottom. He could feel his tail and fins smashing against it, his body bouncing up and down, bumping along the rocks. Finally, the wave let him go, and this time, luckily, he did not suffer any serious injury.

But what had made him lose his concentration?

Had he really seen what he thought he had seen?

It was impossible, so he stared again.

He couldn't believe it. Fifty feet away from him, in the same break, Daniel Alexander Dolphin saw a strange creature riding waves the way he had been doing it throughout his life.

The strange surfer caught a wave and somehow performed the same maneuvers that Daniel had developed in his own reef. The being was different, but the beauty of surfing was the same....

Then he noticed something else. It was not only one creature, but two of them; it seemed that they had come together to share that moment of happiness with the sea, and the way they surfed probably meant that they had been doing it for a long time.

Indeed, these creatures knew how to surf. Having caught a wave, they performed a series of radical maneuvers that would inspire anyone. They knew what they were doing.

So Daniel Dolphin decided to put them to the test. As the next set of waves approached, he caught the first one, dropping vertically and making a radical bottom turn. Immediately, the other surfer paddled and caught the next wave, free-falling in the very late take-off. Daniel performed his best maneuvers before pulling out of the wave. The strange surfer matched Daniel's abilities.

There was nothing else to do, but ask, "So, who are you, and where do you come from?"

There was no answer to Daniel's question, but the two surfers started to talk between them.

"Did you see the dolphin?"

"Sure I saw it. I could swear it was trying to pull the same maneuvers we were performing."

"That's impossible. How could a dolphin learn to do that?"

Daniel felt very annoyed. "Who do they think they are? They should know that I can do much better than this."

And then Daniel Dolphin realized two things. These strange creatures did not know the sonar language dolphins use. While he could understand what *they* were saying, they couldn't decipher the echo signals he was sending.

Daniel also noticed that although there was a certain surprise in their eyes, they were not scared of him; in fact, he felt that he was welcome.

Then the creatures started talking again, while Daniel listened.

"This dolphin must spend quite a bit of time in the big surf."

"Man, if we could breathe the way it

does, then we could probably spend as much time as it does out there."

Beware of the creature called man, Daniel remembered.

He panicked. Those creatures were the ones he had heard about, probably responsible for all the destruction he had seen in his journey. He related the lights on the cliffs to the ones illuminating the black silhouette that seemed to sit on top of the water, killing dolphins and destroying the sea.

"Is this the end of the journey?" he asked himself. "Am I going to die?"

And then, the sea spoke to him:

Where you are
headed there are
no trails, no
paths, just your
own instincts.
You have fol-
lowed the omens,
and have finally
arrived. And
now, you have to
take the great
leap into the
unknown, and
find out for
yourself who is
wrong, who is
right, who
you are.

Something in Daniel's heart was telling him that although he had seen many bad things about this creature called man, he could still trust these two—not because of what they represented, but because he had sensed that for them, surfing was also a way to leave their world in order to pursue their dreams.

Daniel Dolphin had come this far by believing in himself. He had to trust his instincts once more. So he stayed a little longer, sensing that something special was about to happen....

And suddenly, he saw it coming from the west.

The most perfect wave he had ever seen appeared on the horizon. It bent toward the reef, starting to jack-up as it touched the bottom coral, projecting a long, hollow wall of water.

Daniel Dolphin knew that this was the wave he had been dreaming of. He swam to position himself for the take-off. The other surfers saw the wave, too, and they paddled hard to get into position.

They all got into the wave. A vertical drop was followed by a radical bottom turn. Daniel got out of the bottom turn first and projected his body toward the lip of the wave. The other surfers followed him with radical cut-backs and rollers off the white-water. They pushed themselves to the limit, performing maneuvers that they thought they could never achieve. And then, just as the perfect wave started to peel faster, the final section started to break, leaving plenty of space for the surfers to fulfill their dream.

They positioned themselves and fought hard to maintain an edge between bottom and crest, holding their breath....

The lip of the wave slowly wrapped them, deeper and deeper, taking them to a place surfers dream of: the barrel.

It felt as if, for once, the universal language of dreams had prevailed. So this time, not only Daniel Alexander Dolphin, but the other two surfers, understood the meaning of what they had been doing, regardless of where they came from.

And the sea spoke to them:

Some things
will always be
stronger
than time and
distance.
Deeper than
languages and
ways. Like
following your
dreams, and
learning to be
yourself.
Sharing with
others,
the magic you
have found...

Daniel Alexander Dolphin had believed in himself and had followed the omens of his journey. He had finally surfed the perfect wave, and in doing so had discovered the true purpose of his life: to live a meaningful and happy existence by following his dreams. He had crossed the line where dreams become reality, a line that only those who follow their heart can see, and with this new light, Daniel Dolphin saw his life the way it was meant to be; and more than liking it, he loved what he saw....

Daniel spent the next days surfing the reef with the other two surfers. They surfed for the pleasure of doing it, learning from each other, sharing their wisdom.

One day, though, Daniel Dolphin felt that it was time to go back. Now he could return to his beloved island, to where he belonged. He had discovered what he came to discover, and his search was over. It was time to share with the pod the truth he had found.

But what would the other dolphins think, seeing him come back after his alleged death? They would probably think he was some kind of ghost, someone who had returned from the dead.

For Daniel Alexander Dolphin, a dreamer, this would make a funny anecdote. He knew he was a dolphin like any other, but with one big difference: he had chosen to follow his dream by believing in himself.

That afternoon, before Daniel said good-bye to the reef, he spent the most magical surfing session a surfer could imagine in this world. He surfed the same waves with totally different creatures, sharing the same happiness, sharing the same beliefs, knowing that against all odds, they had been right all the time.

Daniel exchanged a final look with his friends, the surfers, and he saw in their eyes the image of his own soul, and he loved what he saw.

He had discovered the real purpose of his life by following his own rules, the ones the pod had told him a thousand times would not work.

He finally discovered that all his achievements, all his aspirations, and all his dreams were now part of his own essence, and he felt good....

Daniel Alexander Dolphin would never forget the day he entered the lagoon of his beautiful island.

It was mid-morning on a warm and sunny day, and in returning to his beloved home after so long, he shed a couple of tears.

The first dolphins to see him almost fainted.

Suddenly, the routine day of the pod started to crumble.

Was that Daniel, the one lost in the outer reef? Wasn't he dead?

Before they could react, Daniel spoke to them. "I have been missing you, my friends..."

"You were dead," someone said.

"No. I was only dead in your eyes. I crossed a line drawn by your own blindness, and that killed me in the name of your Law."

His old friend Michael spoke out. "We thought you were dead, Daniel. No dolphin has gone to the outer reef and returned."

"What do you mean by 'no one,' Michael? Can't you see me? I have gone far beyond the outer reef, and returned. You said it couldn't be done, and yet it *has* been done."

"That's probably because you are special. If any one of us had tried it, then more than certainly we would have failed in our endeavor."

Daniel Dolphin understood that in order to convince them that they were able to do what he had done, he had to show them that dreaming was something they had experienced sometime in their lives, something they had buried in the bottom of their hearts.

"Isn't a dolphin that doesn't follow his dreams a prisoner of his own fears?" Daniel asked.

A whisper spread throughout the pod. The atmosphere was changing, and their initial surprise was dissipating.

"But life is tough enough the way it is now," one of them said.

"Who told you that you have come to this world to suffer? Always dream, and never be afraid."

That morning, Daniel told the pod about his adventures far beyond the outer reef. He told them how he had learned to follow the omens by listening to his heart, and that he had encountered a creature called man who had shown him the good and the evil that dwells within us. But above all, he told them about his dream to find a higher purpose in life and that it had become a reality. And that

he was just a dolphin with the same fears and hopes as any other, but with one difference: he had not given up his dream.

Someone said, "You know that we need to fish in order to survive."

"We all need to stay alive," Daniel said, "and there is nothing wrong with that. So long as we never forget that the reason we fish is to live life to the fullest, to realize our dreams."

"Are you saying that we can be as happy as you are?"

"I am telling you that you can be as happy as you wish. You just have to dream so you can remember who you really are. It is never too late to start again."

"Tell us how to dream, Daniel."

He spoke very slowly. "The real secret of a happy and rich existence is to learn to distinguish between real treasures and false

ones. The sea that embraces us, the sun that gives us life, the moon and the stars that shine in the sky, are all real treasures," Daniel said. "They are timeless, and they were given to us so we could always remember that we are surrounded by magic; to remind us that our world is full of miracles, a world to admire and to help our dreams become reality.

"Instead, we started building our own world of false treasures. We gave up our dreams and accepted that the reason to live was to fish as much as we could."

Daniel became sad. "That's when you stopped dreaming. You denied all the real treasures of life the same way you denied me the day I left for the outer reef. The dream inside you died, and with it all your illusions, all your hope. You forgot how to dream, and it was your only bond with your true self. And it was gone."

Then Daniel asked, "Have you ever seen a dolphin calf look at the sun, the moon, and the stars? He thinks they are magical. You know why? Because in a sense, they are. A calf still dreams, and that is why he can still see things that are magical, things that you cannot see anymore.

"That is what you need to do: dream..."

And that night, finally, the pod remembered. And when they dreamed again, they started to marvel at the world around them, the world that had always been there. So again, the pod found a base from which a happy and fulfilling life could be built.

The next morning, something had definitely changed on the island.

It looked like a normal day in the pod's existence, but a revolution had taken place inside their hearts. Their eyes were shining like stars, and their lives seemed to be much happier.

A new era of hope had begun.

That afternoon, the reef was full of beginners trying to surf; and the ones not surfing were catching the last glimpse of a beautiful sunset.

They had finally found some time to live.

They had remembered how to dream.

Daniel Alexander Dolphin lived a long, fine life. He kept traveling and discovering new worlds, surfing new reefs, falling in love with every sunset, living life to the fullest, always dreaming....

Then one day, he disappeared in the vastness of his beloved sea.

Rumor spread that he was swallowed by a huge wave. He never returned.

But this time, the same dolphins that years before had denied him for violating the Law of the pod, accepted his fate. The seed of dreaming had been sown in their souls, and they knew that one day they would also find the way to turn dreams into reality.

They knew, just as Daniel did, that their journey to the land of dreams had begun.

EPILOGUE

*M*ichael Benjamin Dolphin decided to ride one last wave before returning to the lagoon.

He took off on the first wave of the set. Coming off the bottom of the drop, he crossed the critical section. The wave slowed down, so he had no other option but to cutback and allow the new section to develop in front of him. He stalled with his flipper and waited for the crest of the wave to start peeling over him. The wave wrapped him gently, and for a split second he disappeared in the barrel. Finally, he accelerated clear of the lip, and exited the wave.

It had been a great day of surfing, and he was feeling much better now that he had decided to take time in his life to do the

things he loved and dreamed of.

He started swimming toward the shore, but stopped to watch the beautiful sunset.

His thoughts went back to the past.

He remembered the moments he shared surfing with Daniel, long ago, and how he would spend hours staring at the waves, imagining himself on top of one of those giants walls of water, dreaming.

He had finally rediscovered who he was, the real Michael Dolphin within himself. And it felt good.

"In the world of dreams," Daniel had once said to him, "everything is possible."

Michael stared at the horizon, thinking about his friend.

"Well then," he told himself, "I will find you one day, Daniel, and I will teach you a thing or two about surfing!"

He started swimming back to shore, the

moon high in the sky, the stars shining brighter than ever.

And there, in the vastness of the ocean, Michael Benjamin Dolphin heard the voice for the first time:

There comes a time in life when there is nothing else to do but go your own way...

ABOUT THE AUTHOR

Sergio Bambaren was born in Peru and received a degree in Chemical Engineering from a university in the United States. But above all, he is a surfer at heart. It was his search for the perfect wave that brought him to Australia, where he settled several years ago. *The Dolphin* is Sergio's debut novel.

We hope you enjoyed this Hay House
book. If you would like to receive a
free catalog featuring additional
Hay House books and products,
or if you would like information about
the Hay Foundation, please contact:

Hay House, Inc.
P.O. Box 5100
Carlsbad, CA 92018-5100

(800) 654-5126
(800) 650-5115 (fax)

Please visit the Hay House Website at:
http://www.hayhouse.com